T0128187

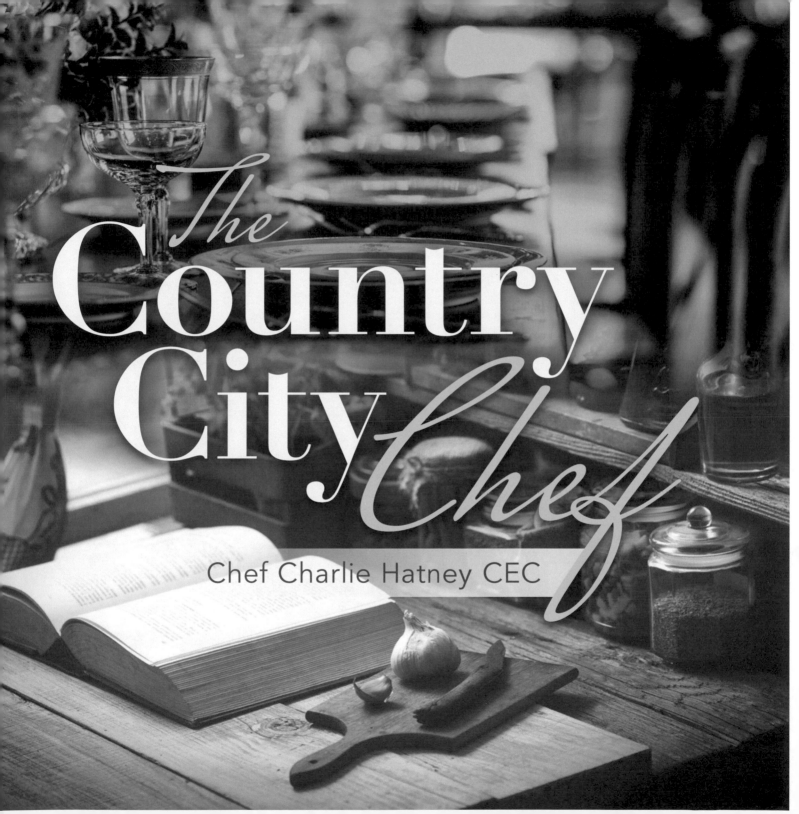

The Country City Chef

Chef Charlie Hatney CEC

The Country City Chef

The Country City Chef

iUniverse
1663 Liberty Drive
Bloomington, IN 47403
www.iuniverse.com
844-349-9409

ISBN: 978-1-6632-1824-7 (sc)
978-1-6632-1825-4 (e)

Library of Congress Control Number: 2021902482

iUniverse rev. date: 02/12/2021

The Country City Chef

Chef Charlie Hatney CEC

To my family, friends, and co-workers

who have lived this book with me and given me encouragement,

to show my skills to the world.

Foreword

Charlie Hatney, Executive Chef, Owner of catering business Hatney & Company, CEO of local nonprofit Mae Homeless Initiative, Board Director of American Culinary Federation, devoted husband, loving father and a friend to all, now presents this cookbook.

Charlie has held several positions in food service. Starting out as a dishwasher and busboy, to a waiter then a cook, and later became an Executive Chef at the age of 28. Under the supervision of Chef Darryl Evans, he became a Certified Executive Chef. Charlie later hosted a scholarship dinner in honor of Chef Darryl Evans. Charlie was a chef for the reelection dinner, hosted by Tyler Perry, for former President Barack Obama and was a chef for No Kid Hungry Give Me Five Dinner. He has served on the board of culinary Rockdale Academy in Georgia and ran a food service program for four months on Seneca Lake in the Finger Lakes region of New York. Charlie has started 3 restaurants, and is now the owner of the successful Hatney & Company. Charlie has been a part of many projects, holding several positions however, what he is most proud of is raising a family with his beautiful wife Angela.

Charlie is a young man who has humbly overcome adversity. Charlie, raised by single mother, was exposed to a number of experiences that would drive him towards his love of the culinary arts. One of his earliest memories was his introduction to Farm to Table. His mother, Johnnie Mae Hatney, would prepare meals from scratch made from foods grown right in her backyard. Her mother, Ruth, raised chickens, pigs, and ducks. They ate fresh the eggs gathered from the chicken coop and fish caught at the nearby ponds. His Grandmother Grace, baked cakes from scratch, including Charlie's favorite upside-down pineapple cake. His Grandfather George Traylor taught him how to harvest potatoes and corn and how to catch, clean and cook fish.

As you can see, Charlie Hatney knows food! This cookbook is full of decadent recipes, sure to make your mouth water, and bring a tear to your eye. No matter your culinary experience, or lack thereof, Charlie's cookbook is guaranteed to make anyone an expert in their own kitchen.

Valyn Reed, *MS, CLC (Nutritionist)*

Table of Contents

Appetizers

Mussels

12 to 13 mussels
1 tsp minced garlic/shallots
1 pinch of parley
¼ cup of white wine
4 oz butter
2 tsp oil blend
5 grape tomato halves

1. Heat pan add oil blend with garlic shallots and mussels
2. Deglaze pan with white wine add all ingredients except butter and salt and pepper.
3. Once wine is reduced slowly add butter and salt and pepper

Blackeye Pea Hummus

12 oz blackeye peas (soaked overnight)
5oz lime juice
4 cloves roasted garlic
3 oz olive oil blend
2 oz cumin
Salt and Pepper to taste

1. Boil the blackeye peas in water until tender, drain and reserve the liquid
2. In a food processor, blend the peas with 3 oz of reserved liquid until it becomes a paste
3. Add all remaining ingredients until well incorporated. Taste and adjust seasonings if needed.

Crab cakes

1-pound jumbo lump Crabmeat

2 large eggs

2 tablespoons of mayonnaise

2 tablespoon Dijon mustard

1 teaspoon Ole Bay

1 tablespoon lemon juice

½ cup sauteed green onions

¼ teaspoon salt and pepper

1 tablespoon tobacco

¼ cup panko breadcrumbs

1. Combine all ingredients to make a mayo. Gently fold in crabmeat and add breadcrumbs with spatula. Careful not shred the crabmeat chunks.
2. Heat pan with vegetable oil form and saute3 minutes per side.

Falafel Hushpuppies

24 oz Cornmeal

16oz Flour 16oz

1 large onion

4 tsp baking powder

2 tsp salt and freshly ground pepper

4 oz vegetable oil

1 tsp cayenne

16 oz buttermilk

8oz ground chickpeas

8 oz chickpea hummus

1. Combine the buttermilk, eggs, oil, onions in a blender
2. Combine all dry ingredients. Add the wet ingredients to the dry ingredients. Combine well then incorporate the hummus and ground chickpeas.
3. Form into round balls or with a one once scoop. Heat oil to 350 and deep fry until crispy and brown.

Curry apple chi...

...mato BLT, spicy mayo

...ella mushroom

Wings Lemon Pepper (grilled or fried)

1 1b chicken wings
2 teaspoon salt and pepper
2 tablespoon melted butter
1 fresh squeezed lemon
2 tablespoon lemon pepper seasonings

1. Heat oven to 375.
2. Season wings with salt and pepper and place in oven for 35 min or 165 degrees
3. Heat butter, lemon pepper seasoning into a pan with fresh squeezed lemon
4. Wings are par baked they can go on the grill or in the fryer and be ready in five minutes.
5. Toss with sauce in bowl and serve

Soups

Corn Chowder

4 oz bacon diced

5 oz diced celery

8 oz diced red and green peppers

5 oz diced yellow onions

2 lbs. fresh or frozen corn

2 lbs. potatoes diced

64 oz corn stock

16 oz heavy cream

2 bay leaves

2 tsp tobacco

2 tsp Worcestershire

1 tsp dry mustard

2 cup blonde roux

1. In large pot render the bacon
2. Add all mirepoix and sweat until softened
3. Add stock to pot and bring to a boil
4. Stir in blonde roux and add potatoes and puree half of the corn and add to the pot
5. Once potatoes are tender and cream and bring to a simmer for 15 minutes.
6. Complete the soup with rest of the corn, tobasco, dry mustard, Worcestershire, and salt and pepper.

Smoked Tomato Soup

8 cups of vegetable stock

5 lbs. of Roma tomatoes cut in half and smoked

1 leek cut into ribbons

2 carrots peeled and diced

4 oz roasted garlic

1 cup of white wine

2 oz olive oil

Salt and Pepper to taste

1. Place oil into hot pot with leeks and carrots.
2. Sauté for 8 minutes. deglaze with wine.
3. Add stock, garlic, and tomatoes and simmer for 30 minutes
4. Puree with a hand blender. Pass through a fine china cap season and serve.

Cream of Mushroom Soup

2lbs portabella mushrooms

2lbs button mushrooms

1 lb. of oyster mushroom

1 lb. Shitake Mushroom

1 cup porcini mushroom powder

1 cup dry sherry

1 gal chicken velouté

1 sachet Epices

18 oz heavy cream

Salt and ground pepper to taste

1. Heat oil and add onion until tender.
2. Add mushrooms reserve 2 lbs. for garnish
3. Add mushroom powder and deglaze with Sherry wine.
4. Add velouté and sachet and bring to a boil and reduce to a simmer
5. Puree Soup and strain.
6. Add the hot cream and season.

Salads

Creole Caesar Salad

1 head of romaine (washed and chopped)
1 oz parmesan cheese
3 ounces baby kale
2 ounces cornbread croutons
2 oz Creole Caesar dressing (basic Caesar dressing with chipotle peppers and Cajun seasonings)

1. Toss all ingredients in a cold metal bowl with half of the parmesan.
2. Finish with remaining parmesan on top

Mixed Green Salad

3 oz Red Oak

3oz Baby Spinach

3 oz romaine

1 oz curry carrots

3 oz tomatoes

3 oz cucumbers

2 oz choice of dressing

1 oz Virgin olive oil

1 tsp Salt and pepper

(meat/egg/olives/cheese to do different variations cobb/chef)

1. Wash and cut greens (spin dry)
2. Toss with virgin olive oil salt and pepper
3. Add dressing and vegetables on top

Roasted Red and Golden Beet Salad

2 roasted red beets

2 oz mixed green

4 roasted golden beets

1 oz golden beet puree

Salt and Pepper to taste

1 oz white balsamic Vinegar

1 oz virgin olive oil

1. Blend 2 golden beet into a puree.
2. Season beets and reserve separately
3. Toss all greens with oil the arrange on the plate.

Summer Tomato & Cucumber Salad

3 Roma tomatoes medium diced

3 cucumbers medium diced

2 red onion medium diced (place in cold water and drain)

Salt and pepper to taste

3 tablespoon apple cider vinegar

1 teaspoon tobasco

1 tablespoon parsley

1tablespoon fresh oregano

1. Combine tomatoes, cucumbers, red onions, herbs, salt and pepper and tobacco
2. Combine vinegar and olive oil in small and whisk together. Add to salad and toss

Entrees

Southern Fried Chicken

1 frying chicken (salt and herb brine chicken overnight)

½ cup flour

1 teaspoon salt

¼ teaspoon freshly ground black pepper

¼ granulated garlic

¼ onion powder

¼ corn starch

1 tsp cayenne

2 eggs well beaten

¼ cup buttermilk

1. Pat dry the chicken free of brine mixture and season.
2. Mix all dry ingredients to flour
3. Add egg and buttermilk to chicken
4. Add chicken to flour and fry at 320 for 12 to 15 minutes.

Blackened Tilapia with Succotash and Jalapeno Grit Cake

2-3 oz tilapia filet

1 teaspoon brown sugar

1 teaspoon chile powder

1 teaspoon paprika

¾ granulated garlic

½ teaspoon dry oregano and thyme

½ teaspoon cayenne pepper

1 teaspoon kosher salt

3 teaspoon unsalted butter

2 cloves of garlic

3 fresh thyme sprigs

½ lemon

1. Place tilapia fillets in large dish and wipe dry.
2. Mix all dry ingredients together to make blackening season.
3. Season fillets and reserve fillets to the side.
4. In large cast iron with oil 2to 2 in a half minutes medium heat sear flesh side down per side.
5. Add fresh thyme, garlic clove, butter and baste the fillets.
6. Squeeze lemon to finish and ready to serve.

Cumin and Fennel Crusted Lamb with White Pepper IceCream

1 rack of lamb

2 teaspoons of salt

1 teaspoon ground black pepper

2 teaspoon cumin seed

2 teaspoon fennel seed

2 teaspoon butter

3 fresh thyme sprigs

2 oz of olive oil blend

1. Clean and salt and pepper rack of lamb
2. Toast cumin and fennel seed. Allow to cool and place in coffee grinder. Add salt and pepper
3. Oil the rack and press spice mixture into the lamb.
4. Heat cast iron skillet and sear lamb on both sides.
5. Add butter garlic clove and thyme and baste the lamb two minutes on both sides.
6. Place on wire rack and finish in oven to desired temperature.

Herb Roasted Chicken w/ Pan Jus

6 lbs. chicken (cut into pieces)

3 teaspoon kosher salt

2 table spoon fresh thyme

1 tsp paprika

2 tablespoon fresh rosemary

1 tablespoon fresh parsley

½ cup minced garlic

3 oz carrot diced

3 oz onion diced

3 oz celery diced

1 quat chicken stock

2 oz corn starch

2 cups vegetable oil

1. Wash, Dry and oil the Chicken
2. Add herbs and cup of oil and refrigerate overnight
3. Heat Roaster pan and sear chicken on both sides
4. Cook 45 minutes to an hour. Check to 180 degrees
5. Remove the chicken and vegetables. Deglaze the pan with white wine
6. Add chicken stock and reduce. Skim top layer of grease. Thicken with cornstarch slurry.

Accompaniments

Southern Collard Greens

Ingredients

1 qt diced onions, .5 cup minced garlic, 1 case kale, 2 case collards, 1 case
5 gal stock, 3 TBL granulated powder, 3 TBL onion powder, 3 TBL crushed red peppers
.5 c black pepper& garlic mix, 1 cup rice wine vinegar, .5 cup sugar, 2lbs smoked turkey legs

Directions

1. In cold water wash and pick kale, wash turnip and collards.
2. Use turkey stock or chicken stock if turkey stock is unavailable. Season stock with garlic powder, onion powder, crushed red peppers salt, black pepper and garlic mix and rice wine vinegar. Add sugar in small amounts until the vinegar is balanced. Set aside.
3. Sauté' onions and garlic in large stock pot until translucent add stock and cover until boiling.
4. Once a rolling boil is reached add greens until pot is full and cover. Boil until greens are all wilted about 1 hour remove from pot and put into 6 inch hotel pans cover tightly with aluminum foil and place in oven.
5. Set timer for one hour intervals and cook for three hours checking for tenderness after the second hour

Southern Rice Pilaf

Ingredients
Butter 8oz
Onions diced 12 oz
Dijon mustard 1 oz
Minced garlic 1 oz
Long grain rice 4 pints
Tomato paste 4 oz
Fresh thyme 2 oz
Chicken Stock 4 ½

1. Heat butter in sauce pan. Add the onion and garlic sauté until it begins to soften with the garlic.
2. Add rice, without washing. Stir over heat until rice is completely covered in butter.
3. Add tomato paste and mustard and stir. Pour in boiling liquid. Return the liquid to a boil and the rice and herbs.
4. Place in 350 degree oven and bake for 20 minutes
5. Fluff with fork and keep hot for service.

Macaroni & Cheese

1 lb. of dried elbow macaroni
½ cup unsalted butter
½ cup all-purpose flour
11/2 cup heavy cream
2 1/2 cups half and half
2 cups of sharp cheddar cheese
1 cup white cheddar cheese
1 cup mozzarella cheese
½ tbsp salt
¼ cup Dijon mustard
3 eggs
½ tsp black pepper

1. Preheat oven to 350 degrees.
2. Bring pot with salted water to boil and add the dry pasta. Cook pasta and reserve.
3. Mix all the cheese together.
4. Heat pan and add butter. Incorporate flout into the butter. constantly whisk until smooth with nutty smell. This is called blonde roux. All the liquid, mustard, whisked eggs,3/4 of the cheese and seasonings.
5. Place in a greased baking dish and bake for 15 min covered.
6. Remove cover and add remaining cheese and bake until golden and bubbly.

Roasted Corn & Fava Bean Succotash

2 pints shelled Fava beans
2 pints white corn
1 pint okra
1 pint vegetable Stock
2 pint heavy cream
1 tsp salt and black pepper
1 pint of diced tomatoes
2 pints green onions
1 lb. of butter
I cup of oil blend

Place cup of oil in sauce pan. Add diced onions and sweat to caramelized. Add Fava beans, roasted corn and okra. Add vegetable stock and reduce. Add cream and butter and salt and pepper to taste. Finish with fresh herbs and diced tomatoes.

Desserts

Peach Cobbler

Filling

10 large peaches peeled and sliced

1 cup brown sugar

4 tsp butter

1 tsp nut meg

1 tsp cinnamon

1 tsp lemon juice

Cobbler Crust

2 cups all-purpose flour

¼ salt

½ cup unsalted butter

1/3 cold water

1. In mixing bowl sift flour and salt.
2. Add butter and crumble together
3. Sprinkle with cold water, mix together and roll into a ball. Refrigerate for an hour.
4. Roll out dough to desired length and thickness.

Banana Foster over French Toast w/ Ice Cream

French Toast

2 eggs
1 Teaspoon vanilla
½ teaspoon cinnamon

½ cup heavy cream
4 slices of challah brad (toasted)

1. Combine eggs, cinnamon, and cream
2. Coat bread on both sides with egg mixture evenly
3. Cook bread in oiled pan on both sides

Banana Foster

4 bananas cut in half then 2-inch pieces
½ of fresh orange
½ teaspoon cinnamon

¼ cup banana liqueur
¼ cup rum

1. Combine sugar, cinnamon, and butter in sauté pan.
2. Add the banana liqueur
3. Add the bananas and cook to they begin softening, add the rum and the squeeze of orange wedge.
4. One banana caramelizes serve with ice cream.

Chocolate Cake

3 once of melted Chocolate

2 1/2 sifted flour

1 ¼ tsp baking powder

½ tsp baking soda

¼ tsp salt

3 large eggs (room temperature)

1 cup heavy cream (Room Temperature)

1 tsp vanilla

8 ounces unsalted butter room temperature

1 ½ cups granulated sugar

1. Pour all dry ingredients into sifter except sugar
2. and set aside
3. Crack eggs and whisk together
4. Combine heavy cream and vanilla
5. Pre heat oven to 350 degrees
6. With mixer cream the butter
7. Add sugar and the slowly incorporate eggs
8. Scape down and add the flour mixture and melted chocolate
9. Spoon mixture into baking pans
   Bake for 35 minutes or until surface bounces back slightly.

Low Country Fair Menu

Gumbo

1 oz vegetable oil

5 oz andouille sausage, small dice

8 oz diced green and red peppers

5 oz diced celery

1/2 oz diced jalapenos

½ once chopped garlic

5 oz cut okra

8 oz diced tomatoes

90 oz chicken stock

2 bay leaves

1 tsp thyme

1 tsp dry basil

2 lb of brown roux

Salt and Ground Pepper to taste

2 lb white rice.

1. Heat oil in pot and add sausage.
2. One it begins to render add vegetables
3. Add stock and bring to a boil.
4. Add the roux and all seasonings except file.
5. Once has cooked about 30 minutes with roux add file and salt and pepper. Top with cooked rice.

BBQ Spiced Shrimp

4- 16/20 shrimp
1 oz BBQ spice (equal parts cumin, brown sugar, kosher salt, smoked paprika, granulated garlic, and chile powder)
2 table spoon unsalted butter
4 springs fresh thyme

1. Heat medium sauté pan with vegetable oil
2. Dust shrimp with spice and add to the pan
3. Once seared on both sides add butter and thyme
4. Baste the shrimp with the butter un shrimp is cooked.

Low Country Boil

3 lbs. crab legs

2 lbs. red potatoes

2 lbs. of kielbasa sausage

4 ears of corn cut in half

2 lbs. of shrimp

2 lbs. of mussels

1 zatarain seasoning packet

4 lemons cut into halves

4 oz crab base

2 lbs. mirepoix (celery. Onion. carrots)

3 oz garlic butter

2 tablespoon ole bay

1. Add three gallons of cold water to large pot
2. Add mirepoix and crab base bring to a boil
3. After one hour remove mirepoix and zatarian bag
4. Add potatoes and sausage cook until fork tender
5. Add the crab and cook for five minutes
6. Add shrimp and mussels for another 5 minutes.
7. Remove from pot add garlic butter and ole bay seasonings

Blackened Salmon w/ Red Beans and Rice

Red Beans
1pound kidney beans (soaked overnight)
cook till tender in salt water and reserve
4 cups of chicken stock
1 medium chopped onion
1 teaspoon spicy mustard
2 teaspoons tomato paste
1 teaspoon brown sugar
1 teaspoon cumin

1 teaspoon garlic
1 teaspoon chile powder
I teaspoon Worcestershire
1 tablespoon hot sauce
I teaspoon paprika
1 tablespoon chopped fresh thyme
2 pounds of andouille medium diced
½ cup olive oil

1. Heat small pot to medium heat and add oil.
2. Add diced sausage, onions and cook with garlic
3. Add tomato paste and stir
4. Add all remaining ingredients cook into beans are thoroughly incorporated
5. Add salt and pepper to taste

Creole Shrimp & Grits

Grits
3 cups of water
1 cup heavy cream
1/3 cup of butter

½ teaspoon salt
½ teaspoon black pepper
¾ cup of grits

Shrimp
½ cup andouille or tasso ham diced
1 pound medium shrimp
1 teaspoon Cajun seasoning
1 oz minced garlic

2 green scallions chopped
3 cherry tomatoes cut in half
3 oz shrimp veloute' sauce

1. In large pot add water , heavy cream, butter and salt and pepper bring to boil. Stir in grits and reduce heat. Cook for 15 minutes and cover. Cook until creamy and smooth texture.
2. In large saute' pan render you diced ham or sausage, Season and saute' shrimp with garlic. Once shrimp is ¾ of the way cooked add bechamel and tomatoes. Finish cooking out the shrimp and garnish with scallions.

Bread Pudding

1 loaf challah bread large dice

6 large croissants diced

20 egg yolks

1 whole eggs

1 cup craisins

1 cup pecans or walnuts

1 cup golden raisins

1 cup of bourbon

2 tablespoon of pure vanilla

3 cups sugar

2 quats heavy cream

1 cup white chocolate chips

1 teaspoon pure vanilla

1. Toast bread and set to the side
2. Combine eggs, cream, sugar, bourbon, cinnamon, and vanilla and whisk.
3. Pour mixture over bread. Allow to soak for 10 minutes.
4. Add choc chips, craisins, nuts, and raisins.
5. Bake on sheet pan for 45 minutes at 350 degrees.

Wine Dinners

Fall

Wines Paired by Chef Nick and Polly Barrington
Caribbean Butternut Squash Soup w/Lobster (Viognier)
Grilled Pork tenderloin w/mango relish and blackberry Ketchup (Petit Chen Blanc)
Creole Caesar Salad with jalapeno corn croutons
(Pinot Gris)
Bread Pudding with Grilled Peaches with Creme Anglaise
(Gamay Beaujolais Nouveau)

Winter

Paired by Lisa Ezzard of The Tiger Mountain Vineyards
Crab and Corn Chowder (Cabernet Franc)
Steak Au Poivre with Pan seared Oysters(Mountain Cyn))
Premium Greens with Chevre (Rose)
Banana Foster French Toast and Bourbon Syrup with Vanilla Ice cream (Sweet Petit)

Spring

Wines Paired by Scott Osborne Fox Run Vineyards
Smoked Tomato Soup (2019 Semi Dry Riesling)
Fennel and Cumin Crusted Lamb with fava bean succotash (2018 Cabernet Sauvignon)
Premium Greens with Brie Cheese (Artic Fox)
Warm Chocolate Cake with Vanilla Sauce (Ruby Port or Old Tawny Port)

Summer

Chef Charlie Hatney of Hatney & Company
Gratin of Lobster Macaroni and Tillamook Cheese (Sauvignon Blanc)(2019 Annia)
Barbeque Spiced Shrimp (Chardonnay)Oberon 2018
Grilled Watermelon and Feta Salad (Sauvignon Blanc) Balletto
Peach Bread pudding with Blackberry Coulis (Merlot) Santa Rosa

Hatney & Company Holiday Menus

Easter Buffet or Mother's Day

Peel & Eat Shrimp with Cocktail Sauce
Champagne Poached Salmon with Traditional Condiments
Assorted Cheese Tray
Assorted Meat Platter
Assorted Cold Buffet Salads
(Carved) Top Sirloin of Beef with Natural Jus
(Carved) Roasted Leg of Lamb with Mint Sauce
Southern Fried Chicken
Smoked Pork Loin with Mango Chutney
Southern Rice Pilaf
Asparagus Polonaise
Vegetable Medley
Seafood Gumbo
Assorted Pastries

Memorial Day, Labor Day or Fourth of July Cookout

Entrée Selections
Grilled Chicken Breast
Hot Dogs
Grilled Hamburgers
BBQ Ribs
Shrimp and Swordfish Brochette
Hot Accompaniments
Baked Beans
Corn on the Cob
Macaroni Salad
Cold Accompaniments
Black Bean and Corn Salad
Coleslaw
Tomato and Cucumber Salad
Watermelon
Lettuce, Tomato, and Pickles
Desserts
Strawberry Shortcake
Seasonal Pies
Ice Cream Sundae w/ Accompaniments

Thanksgiving and Christmas Buffet

Peel and Eat Shrimp with Cocktail Sauce
Poached Champagne Salmon with Traditional Accompaniments
Antipasto Tray
Assorted Cold Salads
(Carved) Roasted Turkey with Turkey Jus
(Carved) Honey Roasted Ham
Fried Chicken
Southern Style Lamb Stew with Polenta
Grilled Swordfish Niçoise
Blackberry Barbecued Loin of Pork with ginger Sweet Potatoes
Mashed Potatoes
Southern Dressing with cranberry sauce
Broccoli with Toasted Sesame and Garlic
Carrots and Honey Pecans
Assorted Pastries

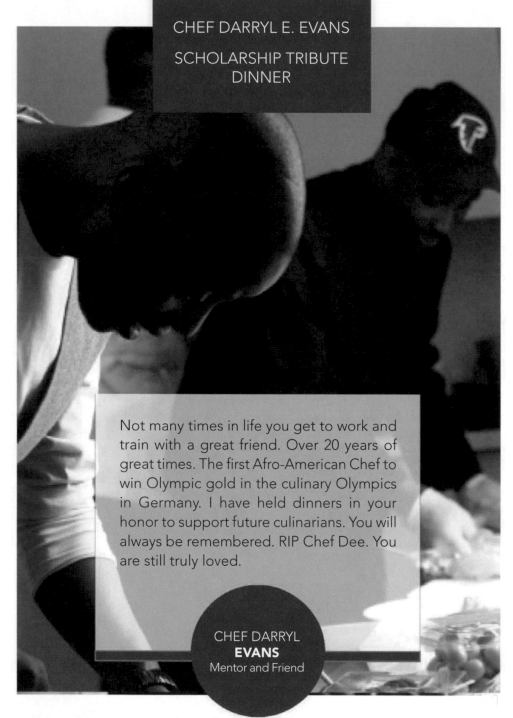

CHEF DARRYL E. EVANS
SCHOLARSHIP TRIBUTE DINNER

Not many times in life you get to work and train with a great friend. Over 20 years of great times. The first Afro-American Chef to win Olympic gold in the culinary Olympics in Germany. I have held dinners in your honor to support future culinarians. You will always be remembered. RIP Chef Dee. You are still truly loved.

CHEF DARRYL EVANS
Mentor and Friend

MAE'S
HOMELESS
INITIATIVE

Mae's Homeless Initiatives (MHI) mission is to strengthen low-income individuals, families and communities by providing quality, safe, decent and affordable housing and nutritional food products and resources. Both the housing and nutritional program serve and support those who are homeless and most vulnerable in society.

JOHNNIE MAE
HATNEY
Mother and Inspiration

Acknowledgments

First, I would like to give thanks to God. He has delivered on his promise. If you have the faith of a mustard seed, you can move mountains.

I would like to thank my Mother Johnnie Mae Hatney. My mother was my rock and a way maker. You left too soon but will always be remembered.

I thank my wife Angela Hatney and my son CJ for allowing me to share my talents with world. The cooking profession is composed of very long hours. It takes a lot to sustain a restaurant.

I thank Greg Johnson. My big brother who watched out for me in my journey in the big city during my teen age years.

I Thank Aunt Elaine,Mary and Aunt Edna an all my family in Augusta for their support.

I Thank George Traylor for teaching me how to be a man and what it takes to make it life.

I thank all my Alabama, South Carolina, North Carolina, Georgia, California, and New York Family.

I thank IHOP Lilburn for giving me a manager job when I lost my restaurant. Most valuable front of the house skills.

I thank Mark Erickson CMC for placing me in the American Culinary Federation for schooling and giving me CIA knowledge.

I thank Chef John Patterson giving me my first shot a becoming a cook from a back waiter.

I thank all the owners who took a chance on me through the years to run their restaurants as an Executive Chef.

I thank Cherokee Town & Country Club for being the base of knowledge for my growth.

I thank Charles and Stacy Bryant family for all the support for me as a young chef.

Thanks to my first cousins who always showed support that wasn't able to see this dream come reality. (Julie Jones and Reggie Bryant RIP

I thank The American Culinary Federation for the support for all these years.

I thank The Hatney Family for their support Dr, J R Hatney, Lois Trotty, Charlie Hatney SR, Wille Hatney, Emogene Battle.

I thank my sister and brothers for all the support through years Erica, Tory, Henry and Rashad.

I thank No-Kid Hungry (Allison Palestrini) for allowing me to be a No-Kid Hungry Chef in The Give Me Five Dinner.

I thank Chef Joe Randall, Chef Nutter, Chef Shular, Chef Wilson, Chef Richards, Chef Anderson, Chef Beals for always having a culinary ear to listen.

I thank Valyn Reed for helping me with this project. could not complete this without you.

Thanks to Mrs. Carolyn Tolbert for all the motherly support from Huntsville, Alabama

The seed money of the people who invested in my non-profit foundation. Here are some of the names. If your name is not listed charge to my head not my heart. (Molly and Leonard Bryant, Constance Lee, Kelvin Snyder, Valerie Cole, Tory Hatney, Greg Johnson, Diane Regular, Polly and Nick Barrington, Louis and Veronica Rodriquez, Joy and Steve Hughes, Valerie Mcdew,

Barbra Shaw, Talesha Crank, Adriene Battle, Dena Hall, Ebony Miller, Leslie Miller, AJ Miller, Elaine and Alwyn Miller, Tiffany Parker, Chris Bee, Erica Hatney, Josh and Julie Anne Bey.

I thank my grandmothers Grace and Ruth for pouring so much love and knowledge into me.

I would like to thank Micheal Wolf and all the Seneca Lake community. I It was a life changing experience. Learning the Jewish community and the love that you share for your community, workers, and each other.

I thank Time to Dine Michelle and Pepper for always having a place to learn and earn while I have pondered my next move in life.

I thank one of the greatest chefs. mentor and friend a person could have Chef Darryl Evans (RIP).

Thank you Uncle Josh and Aunt Juliana Bey for your eye for perfection.

Finally. I would like to thank all the Hatney & Company Customers. I would be nothing without customers enjoying my offerings.

Printed in the United States
By Bookmasters